T0004776

# Supermoto
## Rev it Up!

Brianna Kaiser

Lerner Publications ◆ Minneapolis

Lerner Publications Company
An imprint of Lerner Publishing Group, Inc.
241 First Avenue North
Minneapolis, MN 55401 USA

For reading levels and more information, look up this title at www.lernerbooks.com.

Main body text set in Billy Infant Regular. Typeface provided by SparkType.

**Editor:** Lauren Foley


**Library of Congress Cataloging-in-Publication Data**

Names: Kaiser, Brianna, 1996- author.
Title: Supermoto : rev it up! / Brianna Kaiser.
Description: Minneapolis : Lerner Publications, 2023. | Series: Lightning bolt books. Dirt bike zone | Includes bibliographical references and index. | Audience: Ages 6–9 | Audience: Grades 2–3 | Summary: "In Supermoto, racers compete on different kinds of tracks and face tricky obstacles. Readers will catch an inside glimpse of Supermoto racing and learn about its rules, gear, events, and more"— Provided by publisher.
Identifiers: LCCN 2022006455 (print) | LCCN 2022006456 (ebook) | ISBN 9781728476339 (library binding) | ISBN 9781728478753 (paperback) | ISBN 9781728483306 (ebook)
Subjects: LCSH: Supermoto—Juvenile literature.
Classification: LCC GV1060.1457 .K35 2023  (print) | LCC GV1060.1457  (ebook) | DDC 796—dc23/eng/20220321

LC record available at https://lccn.loc.gov/2022006455
LC ebook record available at https://lccn.loc.gov/2022006456

Manufactured in the United States of America
1-52214-50654-4/20/2022

# Table of Contents

# Time to Race

You race along a flat track and speed up to fly off a dirt jump. Now it's time for a sharp turn. You're in a Supermoto race!

Supermoto is a type of dirt bike race. Dirt bikes are motorcycles that are used only for riding off-road.

Riders racing on an off-road track

# All about Supermoto

Supermoto riders race on both dirt and paved tracks. They also face jumps and other obstacles.

Jumps and obstacles are used in Motocross too. Motocross is another type of dirt bike race.

Motocross racers complete jumps like this one.

Supermoto tracks are usually about 1 mile (1.6 km) long or less, but they can be the size of football stadiums. Tracks have left-hand and right-hand turns.

A Supermoto track leading to a turn

Riders have to follow rules in Supermoto. Rules help keep riders safe. Rules say who is able to compete in an event and what kinds of gear and bikes they have to use.

Rules help riders stay safe in a race.

# Gear Up!

Supermoto bikes are built to handle jumps and sharp turns. They all have similar wheel and rim sizes.

A Supermoto bike in action

The front wheel of a Supermoto racing bike is 21 inches (53 cm) wide. The rear wheel is 18 inches (46 cm) or 19 inches (48 cm) wide.

A rider on a KTM 690 SMC

During competitions, riders have plates on their bikes that show their rider numbers. Some common bikes they ride are the Ducati Hypermotard and the KTM 690 SMC.

Before riders get on their bikes, they have to put on special gear. **The gear helps keep them safe while riding.**

A Supermoto racer wearing safety gear

Riders wear leather jackets and pants. They have upper body armor, including a neck brace and helmet.

Racers wearing special gear and armor

Riders also have knee braces. They wear gloves, goggles, and boots too.

Goggles protect riders' eyes.

# Supermoto Stars and Events

Riders compete in Supermoto competitions across the US and Europe. American rider Dustin Hoffman has won many races, including the 2021 American Motorcyclist

Association (AMA) Supermoto
Championship.

Diego Monticelli has won many
Supermoto races in Europe.
He won the 2020 Supermoto
European Championship.

Monticelli soars into the
air during a Supermoto
European Championship.

Shelina Moreda grew up in California and started racing dirt bikes at the age of 12. She has made Supermoto national rankings nine times. She also competes in other motorcycle races.

Moreda completing a sharp turn in a race

Moreda competes in a motorcycle race.

Moreda works with groups to get more women into the sport. Fans will be able to cheer on new riders in the years to come.

# Bike Diagram
## Ducati Hypermotard

mirrors

engine

tires

# How It Works

Supermoto racetracks have sharp turns. But how do racers make the sharp turns without losing control? Their bikes often have slick tires. The tires on most cars and bikes have grooves in them, but slick tires without grooves are used for dirt bike racing. Their smooth surface grips the ground better than tires with grooves do. This strong grip allows racers to make sharp turns while driving fast.

# Glossary

**armor:** a strong material worn to protect the body

**compete:** to try to win an event

**Motocross:** a type of dirt bike racing where riders compete on a course with obstacles

**obstacle:** a thing, such as a jump, that stands in the way of riders in a race

**off-road:** riding on tracks

**paved:** a hard, flat-surfaced road

**rim:** the part of a wheel that holds the tire

**track:** a special road or course set up for a race

# Learn More

American Motorcyclist Association: Supermoto
https://americanmotorcyclist.com/racing-3
/supermoto

Extreme: MotoX Motocross
https://www.ducksters.com/sports/extrememotox
.php

Hudak, Heather C. *Motocross*. New York: AV2 by
Weigl, 2021.

Mikoley, Kate. *Off-Road Racing*. New York: Gareth
Stevens, 2020.

Motorcycle Racing Facts for Kids
https://kids.kiddle.co/Motorcycle_racing

Slingerland, Janet. *Superfast Motorcycle Racing*.
Minneapolis: Lerner Publications, 2020.

# Index

# Photo Acknowledgments

Image credits: Christian Petersen/Getty Images, p. 4; Jeff Gross/Getty Images, pp. 5, 9; OcMaRUS/Shutterstock, p. 6; Daniel Milchev/Getty Images, p. 7; Stuart C. Clarke/Alamy Stock Photo, p. 8; Phillip Ellsworth/Getty Images, p. 10; NicVW/Alamy Stock Photo, pp. 11, 13; mauritius images GmbH/Alamy Stock Photo, p. 12; Rick Loomis/Getty Images, p. 14; YuryKo/Shutterstock, p. 15; B.Stefanov/Shutterstock, p. 16; Kiko Jimenez/Alamy Stock Photo, p. 17; Zuma Press, Inc./Alamy Stock Photo, pp. 18, 19; Petr Smagin/Shutterstock, p. 20.

Cover Image: AP Photo/Ric Francis.